God Loves Us All...

Big or Little...Short or Tall!!

Nancy Powers and Patricia Powers

Illustrations by Bobbi Switzer

Outskirts Press, Inc.
Denver, Colorado

.

Outskirts Press, Inc.
http://www.outskirtspress.com

ISBN: 978-1-4327-4001-6

Outskirts Press and the "OP" logo are trademarks belonging to Outskirts Press, Inc.

PRINTED IN THE UNITED STATES OF AMERICA

In Loving Memory to
My Hero and Best Friend
My Mom
Pat Powers

To my awesome Dad who showed me
how to triumph over life's tragedies
through ingenuity, persistence, and laughter.
I love you

This Book Belongs to:

It was a dark cool night in the Willowood Forest. The only light was from the bright full moon and the sky full of stars.

The only sound to be heard was….

Swoosh…Swoosh, back and forth shuffling of Mr. Wiggleworm.

He was outside his home anxiously awaiting the birth of his fourth child.

Then it happened, the forest went dark and a loud noise came from inside the house… ooooohhh… POP!

Dr. Thrustout comes out of the house, to speak to Mr. Wiggleworm. "You have a new son, a big boy, and Mrs. Wiggleworm is doing fine."

The Next day…

Mrs. Wiggleworm was awakened by six wide eyes staring at her.

"Can we see the new baby?" asked excited Tina.

"Of course," said Mrs. Wiggleworm.

"You have a new brother."

Willie Jr. looked at him and said"he's not so great."

Tina said "he's beautiful!"

Ike said "Boys are not beautiful!"… Off they went to have their breakfast.

Mrs. Wiggleworm was looking at her new bundle of joy. She noticed his coloring was slightly different then the rest of the family? The new Baby had a fluorescent sheen to him, with little blue specks.

She thought "It will go away with time?" Days and weeks went by and Mrs. Wiggleworm noticed something else was different about the new baby... he was crawling funny? Mrs. Wiggleworm decided to take the new baby to Dr. Thrustout.

The next day Mrs. Wiggleworm took the baby to see Dr. Thrustout.

The Doctor examined the baby and said..."I have some bad news for you Mrs. Wiggleworm. Your baby wiggles when he should waggle and waggles when he should wiggle...actually he has no real wiggle."

As Mrs. Wiggleworm walked home with her bundle of joy, pondering what the doctor had told her, an idea came to her.

Her baby had no wiggle, but was still a gift from God....Sooooo... She would name her new baby...Noah!

Let us all remember...Big or small...Short or tall....

...Wiggle or waggle.

God loves us All!!!

The End

www.ingramcontent.com/pod-product-compliance
Lightning Source LLC
Chambersburg PA
CBHW040309010626
45792CB00025B/1696